Rebel Girls

Dads and Daughters

25 Tales of Teamwork and Fun

Copyright © 2024 by Rebel Girls, Inc.

Rebel Girls supports copyright. Copyright fuels creativity, encourages diverse voices, promotes free speech, and creates a vibrant culture. Thank you for buying an authorised edition of this book and for complying with copyright laws by not reproducing, scanning, or distributing any part of it in any form without permission. You are supporting indie creators as well as allowing Rebel Girls to publish books for Rebel Girls wherever they may be.

Good Night Stories for Rebel Girls and Rebel Girls are registered trademarks.
Good Night Stories for Rebel Girls and all other Rebel Girls titles are available for bulk purchase for sale promotions, premiums, fundraising, and educational needs. For details, write to sales@rebelgirls.com.

This is a work of creative non-fiction. It is a collection of heartwarming and thought-provoking stories inspired by the lives and adventures of 25 influential father/daughter pairs. It is not an encyclopedic account of the events and accomplishments of their lives.

www.rebelgirls.com

Rebel Girls, Inc.
421 Elm Ave.
Larkspur, CA 94939

Text by Alexis Stratton, Jess Harriton, Sydnee Monday, and Shelbi Polk
Art direction by Giulia Flamini
Cover illustrations by Joanne Dertili
Graphic design by Kristen Brittain
Editor: Jess Harriton
Special thanks: Sarah Parvis, Jes Wolfe, Amy Pfister, Eliza Kirby, Hannah Bennett

The authorised representative in the EEA is
Dorling Kindersley Verlag GmbH. Arnulfstr. 124, 80636 Munich, Germany

Printed in China, 2023
10 9 8 7 6 5 4 3 2 1
001-341768-May '24
A CIP catalogue record for this book is available from the British Library.
ISBN: 979-8-88964-110-0

CONTENTS

FOREWORD	4
ALBA AND LUCA TRAPANESE • Content Creators & Disability Advocates	6
ANANYA AND SANJAY SHARMA • Air Force Pilots	8
ÁNGELA AND PEPE AGUILAR • Singers	10
ARY AND JUSTYN HARDWICK • TikTok Creators	12
BINDI AND STEVE IRWIN • Conservationists	14
BRYCE DALLAS HOWARD AND RON HOWARD • Actors & Directors	16
COCO AND COREY GAUFF • Athletes	18
GHAZAL AND QAZI FAROOQI • Motorcyclists	20
GRACEYN AND JAVORIS HOLLINGSWORTH • YouTube Creators	22
JAYDEN AND ROLAND POLLARD • Cheerleaders	24
KATHY AND PETER FANG • Chefs	26
KAWANABE KYOSUI AND KAWANABE KYOSAI • Painters	28
MARINA VASARHELYI-CHIN AND JIMMY CHIN • Mountain Climbers	30
MARY-ANN MUSANGI AND CHRIS KIRUBI • Entrepreneurs	32
MASAYO AND MICHIO HIRAIWA • Wildlife Photographers	34
MONIQUE AND LADI AJAYI • *Race Across the World* Contestants	36
REATA AND BUCK BRANNAMAN • Horse Trainers	38
RILEY KINNANE-PETERSEN AND JOHN PETERSEN • Jewellery Makers	40
SHANEYAH AND SHANE REDSTAR • Singers	42
SMRUTI SRIRAM AND DR. R. SRI RAM • Entrepreneurs	44
SOPHIA AND HAROLD ROBERTS • Heart Surgeons	46
STELLA AND PAUL MCCARTNEY • Fashion Designer & Musician	48
THALMA AND LAÉRCIO DE FREITAS • Musicians	50
XIOMARA ROSA-TEDLA AND DAGNE TEDLA • Entrepreneurs	52
ZAYA AND DWYANE WADE • Model & Basketball Player	54
IT'S YOUR TURN	56
MORE FUN TOGETHER!	58
THE ILLUSTRATORS	61
MORE BOOKS!	62
ABOUT REBEL GIRLS	64

FOREWORD

Dear Rebels,

What are your big dreams? Maybe you imagine yourself as a scientist, inventing new ways to help the environment. Perhaps you picture yourself as an actor in front of a camera. Or maybe you'd like to be a teacher and inspire children every day. When I was a kid, I had big dreams too. I wanted to be an entertainer, and I wanted to train to be an astronaut. Pretty different dreams, I know. But guess what? I got to do both.

As a member of *NSYNC, I travelled the world, singing in front of sold-out crowds night after night. We even performed at the Super Bowl half-time show with one of my all-time favourite bands, Aerosmith! Being a member of the band also afforded me the opportunity to fulfill that other childhood dream I mentioned. I went to Russia and trained with astronauts! Back then, I thought things couldn't get any better. But I had another big dream on the horizon: becoming a dad.

When we got married in 2014, my husband Michael and I knew we wanted to start a family. But as a gay couple, having children came with its challenges. After years of struggle and heartbreak, we finally welcomed our twins, Violet and Alexander, in October of 2021. Now I'm always thinking about what our kids' dreams might be. And as a girl dad – as Violet's "baba" – I want to be as supportive as possible of our daughter.

At just two years old, Violet already has a personality all her own. Her big hazel eyes are always carefully observing everything going on around her. She'll let her brother try out a new slide on the playground before she gives it a go! She's a budding fashion icon and insists on putting together her own outfits, complete with mismatched shoes, layered skirts, and water wings as accessories. It's a look! Michael and I love seeing her little spirit shine. And we want to do everything we can to make sure our Rebel Girl's light never goes out.

I'm so inspired by the ways in which the dads in *Dads and Daughters: 25 Tales of Teamwork and Fun* challenged, encouraged, and supported their daughters. I strive to be the same kind of cheerleader for Violet. Seriously, I will happily grab some pom-poms and a megaphone to cheer my daughter on! And I know that hearing about the accomplishments of all of the amazing women and girls in this book will boost her confidence in a big way. My wish for Violet is that she pursues her passions wholeheartedly and that she never forgets how strong she is.

Every night, I read to my twins, and I've already added the Rebel Girls books to our night-time routine. Violet has been delighted to learn about Zaya Wade strutting down runways with her dad Dwyane beaming in the front row. I know Luca and Alba Trapanese's sweet story about advocating for LGBTQIA+ and disability rights will mean a lot to my family. And I hope reading about Coco and Corey Gauff's journey to tennis superstardom encourages Violet to work hard for her goals.

Get ready to be inspired by all of these amazing stories, Rebel. And know that the person you call dad (or "baba!") is rooting for you, always.

—Lance Bass

BONUS! AUDIO STORIES!

Download the Rebel Girls app to hear longer stories about some of the inspiring duos in this book and discover tales of other trail-blazing women. Whenever you come across a ribbon icon, scan the code, and you'll be whisked away on an audio adventure.

ALBA AND LUCA TRAPANESE

CONTENT CREATORS AND DISABILITY ADVOCATES

Once there was a little girl named Alba who loved to spend time with her dad, Luca. Together, they danced and sang, read books, and played dress up. Their little family was built differently than some, but their happiness felt exactly the same.

When Alba was born, her mother put her up for adoption. But it was a little tricky to find the perfect family for Alba because she had a disability.

Alba was born with a genetic condition called Down's syndrome. Some kids with Down's syndrome have medical problems or developmental delays. People with Down's syndrome are often excellent visual learners and very social. With support, many succeed in school, have lots of friends, and work at rewarding jobs when they grow up.

Enter Luca Trapanese. Luca had a deep desire to be a dad. But strict adoption laws in Italy made it hard for a gay, single man like Luca to adopt a child. Luca refused to give up.

One day, he heard about a baby girl named Alba. Other families didn't think they could care for Alba because of her disability. Luca had volunteered at nonprofit organizations for people with disabilities such as Down's syndrome for many years. He knew he could provide an excellent home for a child with a disability. He immediately applied to adopt Alba.

Luca waited and waited. Finally, he got the call he'd been hoping for – his application was accepted. He was going to be a dad. Luca rushed to the hospital. With trembling fingers, he scooped Alba into his arms. His heart was filled with joy as he looked down into her bright, sparkling eyes.

Today, Luca speaks out for people just like him and Alba – kids with disabilities, single dads, and gay parents – advocating for their wholehearted acceptance.

ALBA, BORN JULY 2017 · LUCA, BORN 14 JANUARY, 1977

ITALY

ANANYA AND SANJAY SHARMA

AIR FORCE PILOTS

Once there was a girl who followed her dreams to the skies.

Ananya knew she wanted to be a fighter pilot from the time she was very little. Growing up on military bases, Ananya saw pilots going to work every morning. Her dad, Sanjay, was one of them. Whenever she heard a fighter jet whiz past overhead, Ananya would stop whatever she was doing and smile. She closed her eyes, imagining her father soaring through the sky. Every evening when Sanjay got home, Ananya would quiz him about all the flights he took that day.

But there was something that confused Ananya. "As a child, I would often ask my father why there were no women fighter pilots," Ananya says. Sanjay always told her not to feel discouraged and to believe in herself. "Don't worry. You will be one," he would say.

Sanjay was right. When Ananya grew up, she joined the military. Every day, she trained and studied to be a pilot. Her father's faith in her abilities helped her keep going even on the days when she thought about quitting.

Then when Ananya was 24 years old, the day came for her and her father to fly their planes in the same formation through the sky. They became the first father-daughter team in the Indian Air Force to fly their planes together. On that unforgettable day, Sanjay thought back to the little girl who gazed up at the clouds, hoping to fly her own plane. He realised that helping his daughter achieve her dream was one of his greatest accomplishments. "That was the biggest day of my life," he said.

ANANYA, BORN 1998 · SANJAY, DATE OF BIRTH UNKNOWN

INDIA

ÁNGELA AND PEPE AGUILAR

SINGERS

Once there was a girl who sang on stage with her family for thousands of cheering fans. Ángela's family concerts weren't like any other show. At an Aguilar show, cowboys rode in on galloping horses carrying Mexican and American flags, dancers in elaborate costumes twirled around the stage, and skilled musicians kept the beat of the lively, traditional Mexican songs known as ranchera.

Ángela herself did more than just sing. She had to manage the flowing skirts of her ball gown while riding a horse *and* delivering soaring high notes. During the show, Ángela wore a tiny earpiece with a direct line to her dad, Pepe. He suggested ways to connect with the audience, and encouraged Ángela during the more challenging numbers.

Ángela felt lucky to have come from a family of singers and performers. She began singing as a toddler. As she grew up, Ángela studied music seven hours a day. She realised that while she loved the traditional Mexican music her father and grandparents performed for sold-out stadiums, she didn't want to do things exactly like they did. "I try to be respectful of what my family has done in the past while still being true to myself," Ángela has said. Pepe supported Ángela doing things a little differently. And he was always there when she needed his advice.

When Ángela started to perform her way — pairing sparkly silver boots with a traditional dress and writing her own songs influenced by pop and R&B artists — fans loved it. Ángela became the youngest woman ever to have a number one hit in Mexico, and she's been nominated for several Latin Grammy Awards. But Ángela is just getting started. She dreams of sharing the music of her heritage with the whole world.

ÁNGELA, BORN 8 OCTOBER, 2003 · PEPE, BORN 7 AUGUST, 1968

UNITED STATES OF AMERICA AND MEXICO

ARY AND JUSTYN HARDWICK

TIKTOK CREATORS

Like many people, Justyn Hardwick found himself spending a lot of time on TikTok in 2020. Simply scrolling through funny videos didn't feel creative, though. *Why not make my own?* he thought. Justyn had some extra free time because of the pandemic anyway. At first, he made videos about gym work-outs or remade sitcom scenes. But then his family got involved.

Justyn's daughter, Ary, started to appear in many of his videos. She'd prank him or come up with clever wagers, like betting him she could finish three large cups of juice before he could finish one. The only catch? He wasn't allowed to touch her cups. He put the cash on the table, and then the game was on! With a twinkle in her eye, Ary started sipping. Then she reached over and covered Justyn's cup with one of her cups. Ary wins!

People began flocking to their page, impressed by how clever Ary was. Now it was Justyn's turn to propose a new challenge. In the video, Justyn sits with a sly grin on his face looking at a bunch of matchsticks laying on the kitchen table. Surely, he would win this time. Ary glides in on a hoverboard, her long braids swinging. "If you can make a square by only moving one match," Justyn said, hiding a chuckle, "you can order something online."

Her rapid-fire problem-solving skills went into high gear, as she took a moment to think. Ary moved a match, and the ends of the sticks formed a tiny square. She rolled back out as swiftly as she came in, only now a toy richer. "Like a boss," one viewer commented.

With videos like that one, the Hardwicks have gained over half a million followers. They're proud to bring a little more laughter to people's lives with their fun-loving, brain-teasing challenges.

DATES OF BIRTH UNKNOWN
UNITED STATES OF AMERICA

BINDI AND STEVE IRWIN

CONSERVATIONISTS

Once upon a time, there was a girl named Bindi who grew up surrounded by wild things at her family's zoo in Queensland, Australia. When Bindi was a newborn, her dad Steve proudly introduced her to all the animals. Bindi grew up making friends with geckos and snakes. She hand-fed birds and snuggled koalas. And when she went to bed at night, her dreams were filled with crocodiles lying in the sun and kangaroos jumping about.

Together, Bindi, Steve, Bindi's little brother, Robert, and her mum, Terri, crisscrossed the globe going on adventures while Steve filmed movies and TV shows about nature. Steve was famous for his love of animals, and people everywhere knew him as the Crocodile Hunter. He didn't hunt crocs, though— he helped protect them. And through his TV shows, he taught people to love wildlife as much as he did.

Bindi took Steve's lessons to heart. Once, she even donated her tooth-fairy money to a koala hospital. Another time, she convinced her parents to save a leech because it was part of nature too!

Soon, Bindi was guest starring on her dad's TV show – and she seemed destined to follow in his footsteps. But when Bindi was eight years old, something terrible happened. Her father passed away. Bindi was devastated, and she missed him every day. But as she wandered through the zoo, gazing at all her animal friends, she knew he would always be with her.

Now in her 20s, Bindi works at the Australia Zoo with her family. Clad in khaki like her dad used to wear, she teaches people to protect nature. With each animal she helps, she carries on Steve's dreams – and her own.

BINDI, BORN 24 JULY, 1998 · STEVE, 22 FEBRUARY, 1962 – 4 SEPTEMBER, 2006

AUSTRALIA

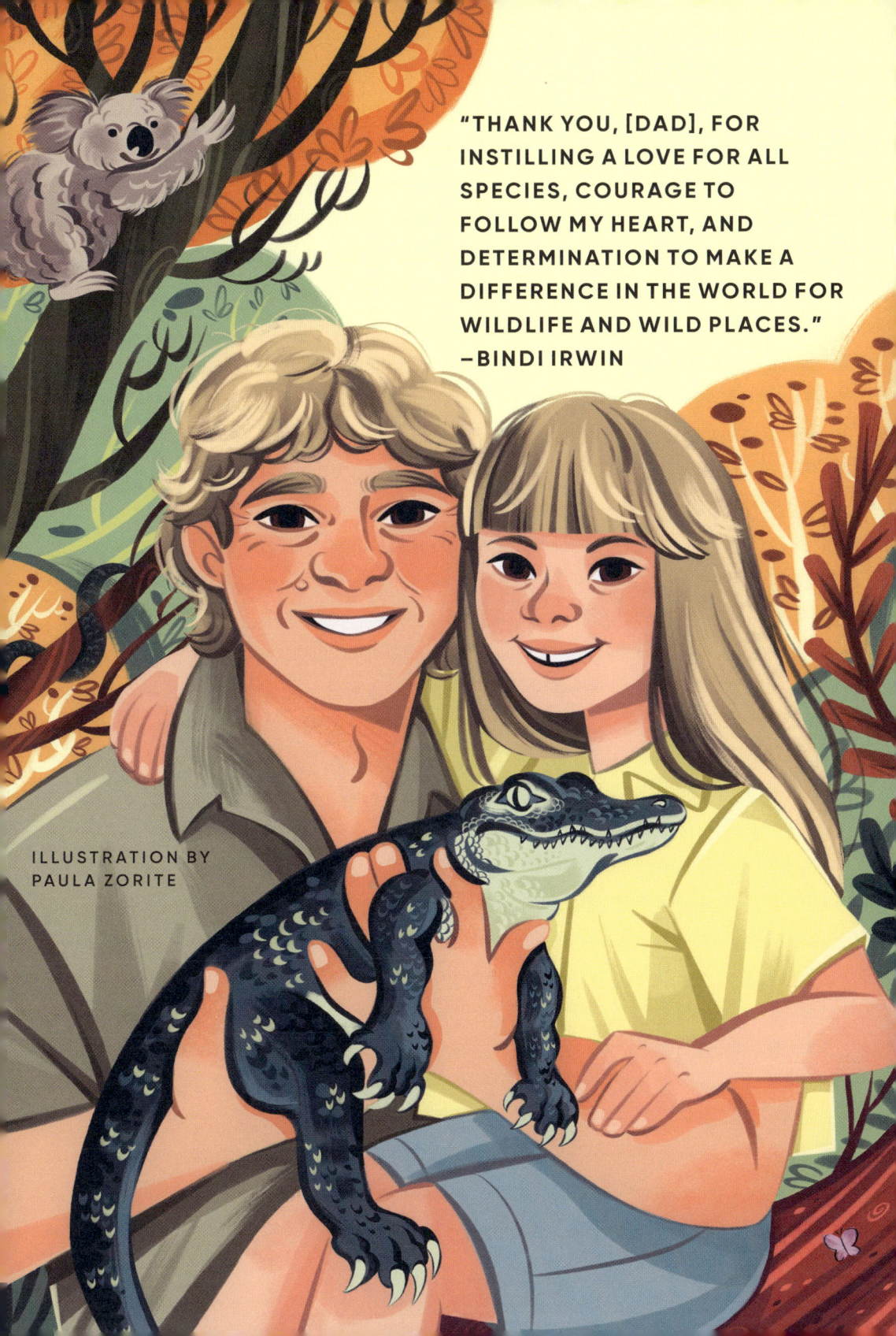

BRYCE DALLAS HOWARD AND RON HOWARD

ACTORS AND DIRECTORS

Once there was a little girl who loved to pretend. But instead of trying on princess dresses, Bryce got to use her imagination on real film sets. Her dad, Ron, was a director, and Bryce was a regular on his sets, either behind the scenes or in front of the camera as a smiling, red-headed extra. She loved it all: the lights, the costumes, the thrill of her dad calling "Action!"

Ron understood her excitement. He too grew up on film sets. Ron began acting on a popular sitcom when he was six years old. He delighted in sharing his passion for filmmaking with his daughter. But he also preferred to keep his family out of the spotlight. Bryce and her three siblings grew up on a rolling green farm in Connecticut, worlds away from the glitz and glamour of Hollywood. On their drives to school, Ron would tell Bryce about the scripts he was reading featuring mermaids falling in love, astronauts in space, and aliens making their home in a swimming pool. There was nothing that lit up Bryce's brain more than storytelling.

After secondary school, Bryce went to college in New York City. As she studied filmmaking and auditioned for roles, she replayed the memories of her director dad on set when she was younger. "I don't think he realised that I was kind of like a computer, taking everything in, and how much that would add up over time," she said.

Add up it did. Bryce took her experiences growing up with her dad to build her own successful career in Hollywood as an award-winning actor and director. Now she's the one calling "Action!", and Ron is first in line to watch the stories she brings to life.

BRYCE, BORN 2 MARCH, 1981 · RON, BORN 1 MARCH, 1954

UNITED STATES OF AMERICA

COCO AND COREY GAUFF

ATHLETES

At 15 years old, Coco stood on the bright green grass of No. 1 Court at Wimbledon, the oldest tennis tournament in the world. The biggest match of her career was about to begin. Crowds filled the stadium, and on the other side of the net was her idol, Venus Williams.

Coco couldn't believe she was there. She had started playing tennis at six years old. Her dad, Corey, was her head coach. Every day, they went to the courts together to practise. And at every match, he sat in the stands with Coco's mum, cheering her on.

It wasn't always easy. Coco was home-schooled so she could travel to tournaments. She missed going to school and being around other kids. But more than anything, she loved tennis. She was determined to go pro, and Corey was determined to help her get there.

In 2019, Coco was ranked number 313 among women tennis players. She wasn't ranked high enough to automatically qualify for Wimbledon, but she won a wild-card spot. Her stomach flip-flopped as she imagined playing Venus. Before Coco stepped onto the court, her dad pulled her aside.

"Keep it simple," he said, "and stay in the moment."

As Coco sent the ball whizzing across the court with her powerful two-handed back-hand, she pretended Venus was not one of the most famous women players in the world. Instead, Coco imagined herself on a court back home in Florida, playing against her dad.

Coco bounced on her feet, scoring again and again. In the final set, she drove the ball hard across the court — and Venus sent the ball into the net.

Coco couldn't believe it. She won! Beaming, she looked into the stands. There was her dad, pumping his fists and cheering for her — as he always did.

COCO, BORN 13 MARCH, 2004 · COREY, BORN 16 AUGUST, 1971

UNITED STATES OF AMERICA

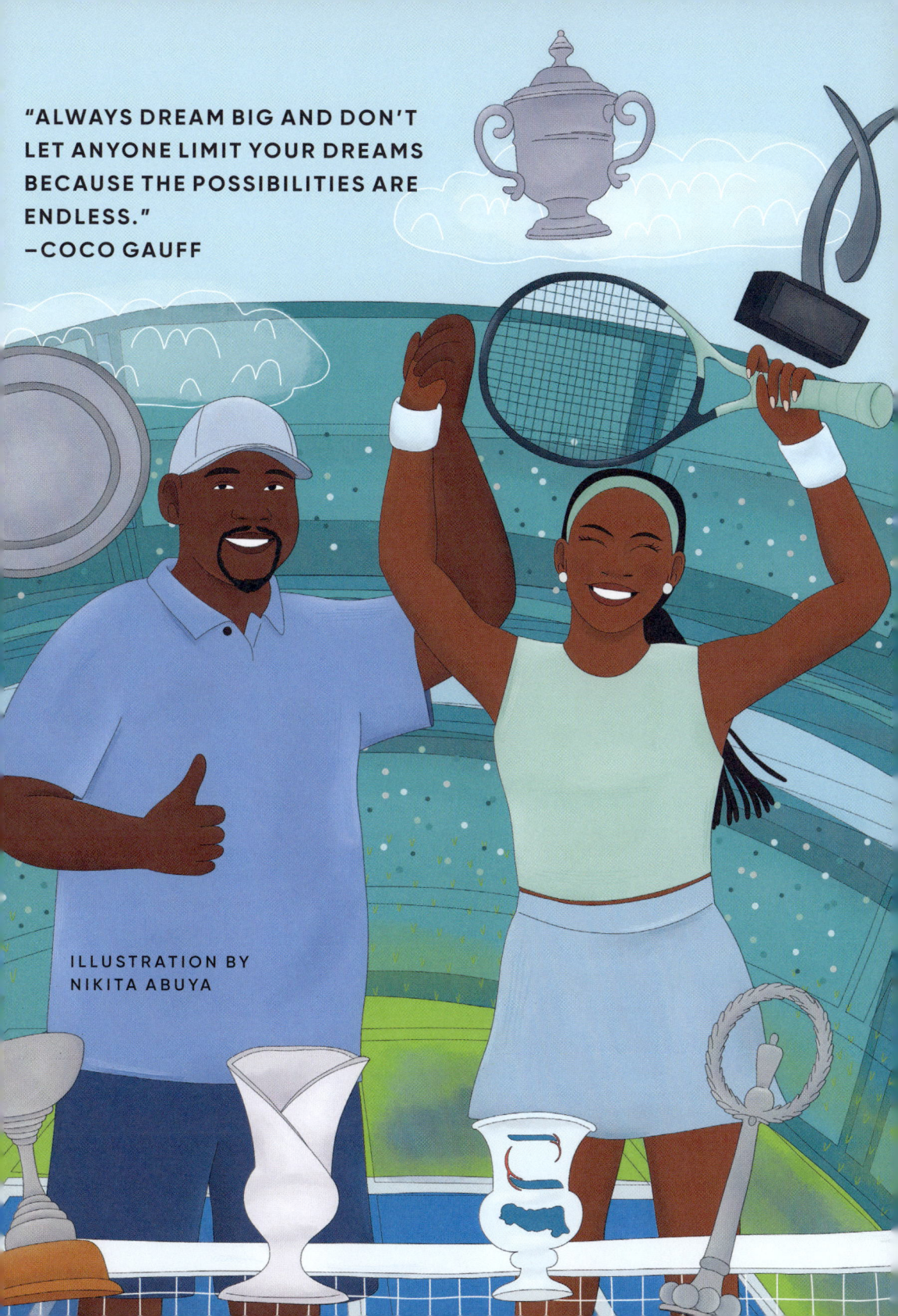

GHAZAL AND QAZI FAROOQI

MOTORCYCLISTS

When Ghazal was a little girl, two of her dad's friends pulled up to her house on motorbikes. The pair were on a bike trip through Pakistan, zooming through the mountains and countryside. Ghazal couldn't think of anything cooler. *That*, she thought, *is how I want to see my country.*

Ghazal's dad, Qazi, rode a motorbike instead of driving a car any chance he got. He was thrilled to see Ghazal's interest and got her a scooter to practise on. But some people in their community didn't think girls should ride at all. Ghazal could feel disapproving eyes watching her. She had her father's support, though, and that was all that mattered.

As Ghazal grew up, she took on more challenging rides, like Shimshal Valley Road — one of the most dangerous roads in the world. The narrow, gravel path winds through tall mountains, and there's no barrier to protect riders from the steep drop over the edge. During that ride, Ghazal's bike skidded, and she nearly slid off the road! Ghazal righted her bike just in time. Her heart skipped a beat, but she was OK.

Today, Ghazal and Qazi's favourite way to spend time together is motorcycling through Pakistan, often for weeks at a time. Every morning, Ghazal pulls on thick padded clothes, double-checks her camera, and tightens her helmet. Then, with the *vroooom* from their engines, she and her dad are off!

Not only did Ghazal achieve her dream of motorcycling through Pakistan, she also found a supportive community worldwide when she began sharing videos of her adventures online. Now she gets to show off the beauty of her home to tens of thousands of followers. Some people still disapprove, but Ghazal and her dad leave those people in their rear-view mirrors.

GHAZAL, BORN 23 JANUARY, 1992 · QAZI, DATE OF BIRTH UNKNOWN

PAKISTAN

GRACEYN AND JAVORIS HOLLINGSWORTH

YOUTUBE CREATORS

When the COVID-19 pandemic hit, the Hollingsworth household came to a halt, along with the rest of the world. Graceyn and her brother and sister stopped going to school, and their parents stopped going into work. Since Graceyn's science professor dad, Javoris, now taught from home, he couldn't help but pay more attention to the content on his children's tablets. He noticed that there weren't many characters on Gracie's favourite shows who were Black like her.

After a couple of months of staying inside, everyone was bored. And Javoris was tired of hearing the same songs and seeing the same animations on his daughter's screen. Growing up, he had loved playing keyboards at church. *Maybe*, Javoris thought, *we can create something amazing even during this difficult time.*

Javoris hypothesised that he and Gracie could pair her knowledge of children's content with his musical abilities to address the lack of representation. Their biggest experiment to date was born: a YouTube show called Gracie's Corner!

Javoris sat behind his laptop, making rhythms inspired by hip-hop and Afrobeats. Gracie joined him, singing along with her headphones on. Together, they put their own spin on old nursery rhymes and made entirely new songs too. Then they matched the songs to colourful animations featuring characters that had brown skin like their family did. Their videos got millions of views. But for Gracie and her dad, creating together is what's really meaningful. "It's just been so fun spending time with my dad, while also making the music," Gracie says. "I've been enjoying this journey."

GRACEYN, BORN 7 AUGUST, 2012 · JAVORIS, BORN 11 JULY, 1985

UNITED STATES OF AMERICA

JAYDEN AND ROLAND POLLARD

CHEERLEADERS

At six months old, Jayden Pollard learned to fly. At least, that's what it felt like.

Even before Jayden could walk and talk, she was doing cheerleading stunts with her dad, Roland. With each lift, Jayden squealed with delight. Roland was a professional cheerleader and coach. He could do back-flips and twirls in mid air. And when Jayden was born, Roland knew he had a new stunt buddy.

As she grew, the moves got more daring. Soon, Jayden was standing tall on her dad's right hand as he lifted her towards the ceiling. She raised her arms in a V and pulled one knee up, balancing on one foot. Up high, in their living room, Jayden delighted in looking at the small world below.

Then, at her dad's signal, Jayden jumped off her dad's hand, falling briefly through the air, before he caught her safely in his arms.

Sometimes he spun Jayden around on one hand. Other times, he flipped her skywards. Jayden was brave, but she got scared sometimes too. It was hard to learn new moves, like twisting in the air or being lifted out of a handstand. But she trusted her dad. So no matter how challenging a move was, she tried until she got it right.

One day, Roland shared videos of the stunts he and Jayden did together on social media so his friends could see. Their gravity-defying routines were so captivating others started watching them too. Soon, Roland and Jayden had millions of fans all over the world!

Roland was a pro, and Jayden was a natural. But more than anything, Roland loved seeing his daughter feel accomplished and confident, and Jayden loved to fly. She knew her dad would be there to catch her.

JAYDEN, BORN 22 FEBRUARY, 2016 · ROLAND, BORN 23 AUGUST, 1990

UNITED STATES OF AMERICA

"CHEERLEADERS ARE SUPERHEROES."
—ROLAND POLLARD

ILLUSTRATION BY ALLEANNA HARRIS

KATHY AND PETER FANG

CHEFS

Kathy Fang grew up surrounded by the tantalising smells and sights of her parents' cooking. Their restaurant, House of Nanking, was Kathy's second home. After school, she would do her homework there in between chatting with the customers. Sometimes Kathy's parents worked late into the night, and she would find a spot to curl up and fall asleep. Her dad, Peter, would carry her home.

When Kathy got a little older, her dad taught her how to cook in the restaurant's kitchen. Kathy loved methodically chopping spring onions into small pieces. She delighted in the smell of sliced ginger and diced garlic. And she was inspired by the smiles she saw on the customers' faces as they took their first bites.

Peter and his wife, Lily, opened House of Nanking in 1988 — shortly after they immigrated from Shanghai, China, to San Francisco, California. As the years went by, Peter became famous for putting new twists on classic dishes, such as adding peanut sauce to dumplings, and customers lined up around the block. House of Nanking became a must-visit destination in San Francisco's Chinatown.

When Kathy graduated from secondary school, she studied business and got a job in an office. But Kathy was miserable sitting at a desk all day. She wanted to be creating delicious meals in a kitchen.

So Kathy went to culinary school in 2006. Like her dad, Kathy excelled at adding unique touches to traditional dishes. She became a skilled and creative chef. In 2009, Kathy opened a restaurant with Peter called Fang. Today, they continue to invent new recipes together at Fang and the always popular House of Nanking.

KATHY, BORN 27 FEBRUARY, 1982 · PETER, BORN 10 FEBRUARY, 1949

UNITED STATES OF AMERICA AND CHINA

KAWANABE KYOSUI AND KAWANABE KYOSAI

PAINTERS

Once there was a girl who giggled as she copied her father's funniest paintings. People came from all over the world to visit or study art with Kyosui's father, Kawanabe Kyosai. He created serious portraits of famous Buddhist monks and beautiful illustrations of Japanese folk-tales. But the ones Kyosui loved the most were his long scrolls of ancient comics with silly scenes of monsters and ghosts learning their lessons in a rowdy classroom.

Kyosui didn't have to wait until there was an opening in one of Kyosai's classes. She got to make art with her dad every single day. Together, they carved tiny, detailed figures and scenes into blocks of wood that they used like giant stamps. The pair coated the woodcuts in ink and pressed them onto paper. They groaned together when a print came out smudged and smiled broadly when they got a perfectly crisp image.

When Kyosui was growing up, it was unheard of for girls to study art. Kyosui was grateful to have a dad like Kyosai who supported her dreams of becoming an artist. She didn't take her opportunity to learn for granted. Like her dad, Kyosui mastered many different styles of painting and printmaking and became a well-known artist. She painted vivid pictures of women and children, devotional Buddhist images, and scenes from her favourite plays. She even made some funny pictures, just like her favourite of Kyosai's.

When Japan's first art school for girls opened in 1900, Kyosui was so excited. She was ready to share all the knowledge her father had shared with her. Kyosui became one of the school's first teachers. She inspired a new generation of girls to pursue their dreams — just as her dad had done for her.

KYOSUI, 4 JANUARY, 1868 – 7 MAY, 1935
KYOSAI, 18 MAY, 1831 – 25 APRIL, 1889

JAPAN

ILLUSTRATION BY
PEILIN LI

MARINA VASARHELYI-CHIN AND JIMMY CHIN

MOUNTAIN CLIMBERS

When Marina Vasarhelyi-Chin was seven years old, she looked out of the windows of her home in Wyoming and pointed to a rugged peak in the distance.

"I want to climb the Grand," she proclaimed.

"You want to climb *that*?" her dad, Jimmy, asked. "It's pretty big."

The Grand Teton *was* big – 4,198 metres feet tall to be exact. But Marina's dad was a professional mountaineer, and Marina had been adventuring with him for years, from surfing big waves to skiing down snowy slopes. Still, even skilled adults hesitated to climb the Grand. But Marina asked her dad again and again, all summer long. Finally, he relented.

In September, Jimmy and Marina hiked to the base of the Grand. As they trekked, Jimmy told Marina stories of mountain dwarves and enchanted springs. She imagined magical creatures traipsing through the woods and smiled.

Marina smiled a lot, in fact: when they camped in a breezy tent at the foot of the mountain, when they strapped on their safety gear, when her fingers first touched the cool, rough face of the rocks. She loved it all.

But about halfway up, her smile faded. She was exhausted. Her dad said they could go back down, but Marina shook her head. Instead, she curled up in a nook on the mountainside, the sun warming her skin as she napped.

When Marina woke, she was ready to face the rest of the climb. "Take it one step at a time," Jimmy said. And she did. Hours later, they reached the summit. As Marina pulled herself onto the peak, joy bubbled up inside her. She'd done it! Jimmy gave her a big hug. Then they stood on the mountain top together, staring out to the horizon, looking towards adventures to come.

MARINA, BORN 25 SEPTEMBER, 2013 · JIMMY, BORN 12 OCTOBER, 1973

UNITED STATES OF AMERICA

MARY-ANN MUSANGI AND CHRIS KIRUBI

ENTREPRENEURS

Ever since she was young, Mary-Ann had a knack for business. She was often dreaming up business ideas, like selling yummy snacks at her school in Kenya. It came naturally. Her dad, Chris, was always going in and out of meetings. Sometimes, little Mary-Ann would march into her dad's office, pull him out of his chair, and take the seat behind the desk.

"I'm the boss," she would say. Nothing made Chris smile more.

It wasn't until Mary-Ann was older that she understood that her dad ran an empire — with investments in technology, media, and real estate. When she became an adult herself, Mary-Ann worked at different corporations before deciding to run a business of her own. She started a restaurant called Secret Garden in Nairobi. Day or night, customers could enjoy their meals in the restaurant's leafy courtyard.

But in 2018, things changed. Chris was diagnosed with cancer. Mary-Ann started to help out at his company more often. She would sit in on meetings during the day, and in the evening, when her father invited his colleagues for dinner, she'd volunteer to help out. During those dinners, Mary-Ann learned valuable tips. She often saw him managing difficult situations and took mental notes about how he would negotiate with others to achieve his goals.

For the next three years, Mary-Ann became closer to her father's colleagues. They built plans for the company and built trust with one another. And then, in 2021, Chris passed away. It was time for Mary-Ann to step into his shoes. As she looked back on her life with her father, she remembered that she hadn't just been preparing to run his empire the last few years — she had been training for this all her life.

MARY-ANN, BORN 14 MARCH, 1971 · CHRIS, 20 AUGUST, 1941 – 14 JUNE, 2021

KENYA

MASAYO AND MICHIO HIRAIWA

WILDLIFE PHOTOGRAPHERS

Growing up in Japan, Masayo Hiraiwa listened in wonder as her father, Michio, told stories of his travels far and wide. What she loved most of all were his beautiful black-and-white photos from his trips to Kenya.

Michio was a journalist who worked for newspapers and magazines. In 1972, British Airways opened a flight between Tokyo, Japan, and Nairobi, Kenya, and Michio was invited on a press tour.

Michio instantly fell in love with the wildlife and culture of Kenya. He took photos of cute baby elephants, frolicking giraffes, and playful monkeys. He hiked through the desert and explored cities. He dipped ugali — a type of porridge made from maize flour—into rich, savoury stews and ate with joy.

One day on the tour, Michio was stressed about running late. But an older Kenyan man told him, "*Pole pole,*" which is Swahili for "take it easy." Michio realized the Kenyan man was right. *You only live once*, he thought, *so why hurry?*

For Michio, that trip changed everything. When he returned to Japan, he cut back his workload by half. He told his family, "We're going to lead a pole pole life."

After that, his family spent more time relaxing and having fun. Over the next 40 years, Michio traveled to Kenya more than 150 times — and Masayo joined her dad for 138 of those trips. Together, they wrote and published guide-books and arranged tours for Japanese travellers. Eventually, both Michio and Masayo were named Goodwill Ambassadors of Kenya and its neighbouring country Tanzania.

In 2015, Michio turned 80. With his daughter Masayo at his side, he celebrated his birthday on the savannahs of the Serengeti, eating delicious East African food while surrounded by incredible wildlife and his Kenyan and Tanzanian friends.

MASAYO, BORN 1960 · MICHIO, BORN 1935

JAPAN

MONIQUE AND LADI AJAYI

RACE ACROSS THE WORLD CONTESTANTS

Ladi knew from the moment his daughter Monique was born that he would always be by her side. So when Monique decided she wanted to trek over 10,000 miles through Canada as a contestant on a TV show called *Race Across the World*, all he asked was what he needed to pack.

The rules of the show were simple: no credit cards, phones, or air travel. The first pair to get from Vancouver, Canada, to St. John's, Newfoundland, would win. The duo knew it was going to be a challenge. But with Ladi's helpful wisdom and Monique's boundless energy, they believed they had a pretty good chance of winning the $24,000 (about £19,000) prize. So, in the autumn of 2022, they packed up their backpacks, laced up their hiking boots, and set out on their adventure.

The journey was tough. Canadian hospitality sometimes helped out along the way – strangers offered directions and some gave them rides to the check-points on their journey. Other times, all Monique and Ladi had were each other. At one point, to save money, the two ate a meal of just tomato sauce and mustard sandwiches! But the real scare came when Monique and Ladi encountered a baby grizzly bear in one of Canada's national parks. They knew a protective mama bear wouldn't be too far behind. The park had closed for the day, so they had to rely on the show's emergency crew to shuttle them to safety.

Side-by-side, through the silent wilderness and bustling cities, they talked and joked and listened to Ladi's favourite tunes on his old iPod. They hadn't been able to spend so much time together since Monique was a kid. So when they came in third place, it wasn't a disappointment. They may not have won the prize money, but the memories they created together were priceless.

MONIQUE, BORN 6 APRIL, 1997 · LADI, BORN 17 JUNE, 1969

UNITED KINGDOM

REATA AND BUCK BRANNAMAN

HORSE TRAINERS

Once upon a time, there was a little girl who braided her pony's mane while her dad, Buck, taught horses and their owners how to trust each other. At first, the skittish horses would kick up clouds of dust and whinny in protest. But by the end of their time with Buck, they would be calm and ready to let their humans take the reins. Reata had already learned how to take good care of her pony from her dad, but she still listened to every word of his lessons.

When she got older, Reata learned that her dad didn't feel safe when he was a kid. His dad was so loud and mean that Buck had to live with a foster family. Buck's foster mum, Betsy, made him feel loved for the first time. As he grew up, Buck noticed that some people treated their horses like his dad had treated him. He became a horse trainer to create better bonds between animals and their owners. Most of the time, Buck trained the humans just as much as the horses!

Reata always knew she was loved growing up — and she and her family extended that same care to their animals. On their sprawling ranch in Wyoming, she and Buck fed their horses fresh hay, cleaned their hooves and stalls, and practised swinging a lasso under the setting sun with the mountains in the distance. The work came naturally to Reata. In college, she even started teaching classes on caring for horses, making her the school's youngest instructor ever.

Today, Reata and her family live on the same farm where her first pony was raised, and she's training a new generation of ranchers. Reata is so proud to share the same career as her trail-blazing father. "My dad is the best there is," she says.

REATA, BORN 30 MARCH, 1995 · BUCK, BORN 29 JANUARY, 1962

UNITED STATES OF AMERICA

RILEY KINNANE-PETERSEN AND JOHN PETERSEN

JEWELLERY MAKERS

Once upon a time, there was a girl named Riley who loved sparkly things. When Riley was a toddler, her dads, John and William, created a treasure-chest for her full of shiny necklaces and jangly bracelets. They gathered the trinkets and baubles from second-hand shops and friends. Riley spent hours sifting through the jewels and finding the perfect pieces for her dress-up outfits. As Riley got older, John took the jewellery Riley cast aside to make unique pieces of his own.

After dinner each night, John sat at a big table under a bright light, cutting apart links from necklaces and fastening on crystals and metal pieces. Riley often sat beside her dad, watching him work and asking lots of questions.

One day, when Riley was five, she said she wanted to make something too. So John taught her how to use pliers to pull apart chain links. He showed her how to hold the tweezers just right. He taught her how to tie snug knots. John encouraged her to experiment with ideas, and Riley quickly developed her own sense of style, full of colourful beads, playful pom-poms, and glittering charms.

John sold his necklaces through his online store named Gunner & Lux and his social media accounts. Riley began selling her jewellery at a lemonade stand in front of their house. Her designs sold well and Riley asked to add her necklaces to John's website. People loved her creations, and they quickly sold out. Soon the website was devoted exclusively to Riley's pieces.

Now at 14, Riley is Gunner & Lux's creative director — and her dad's boss! She still sketches and designs each piece — from rainbow necklaces to snail earrings. Through her whimsical designs, she hopes everyone feels empowered to express themselves with fashion, just like she does.

RILEY, BORN 29 AUGUST, 2009 · JOHN, BORN 20 JUNE, 1977

UNITED STATES OF AMERICA

SHANEYAH AND SHANE REDSTAR

SINGERS

Shane Redstar belongs to the White Bear First Nation. As a composer and singer, one of his favourite things was playing Indigenous songs at community gatherings with his daughter Shaneyah close by. Then the 2020 Covid-19 pandemic hit — and the music stopped. Everyone had to stay inside. After several weeks in their home in Canada, Shane noticed that Shaneyah was beginning to mope around the house. She missed her friends and the connection she felt with her community.

Shane wondered if music could help her feel better. So one day, he brought out his hand drum and asked if she would like to sing. Playing music together felt inspiring. *Maybe we can boost other peoples' spirits too*, they thought. After practising a few times, Shane and Shaneyah began sharing videos of their music online.

Together, they would go down to a nearby lake and stand in the grass under tall green trees. Shane melodically hit the drum and sang while Shaneyah kept the pattern of his rhythm with her feet. Stomping, she slowly added in her high-pitched harmonies with uplifting lyrics like: "Listen to the wind in the willows, telling you 'Yes, it's true, I love you.'" More and more people began to watch and comment on their videos. From there, they began to enter singing contests. They even landed a recording deal!

Shane and Shaneyah are so proud their pandemic hobby turned into a way for them to share their heritage and connect with others. As their voices harmonise to the beat of the drum, they connect to their lineage, one song at a time.

SHANEYAH, BORN 6 SEPTEMBER, 2012 · SHANE, BORN 2 JUNE, 1980

CANADA

SMRUTI SRIRAM AND DR. R. SRI RAM

ENTREPRENEURS

Once there was a girl who never called her father "dad"... at least not at work.

Growing up, Smruti's dad, Sri, slipped lessons about taking risks into their bedtime conversations. At the park, Smruti overheard him networking with the other parents. His company, Supreme Creations, replaced plastic shopping bags with eco-friendly options. Smruti knew her dad was smart and determined. But as she got older, Smruti realised being a successful entrepreneur was rare. She admired her dad's bravery.

That's why, after university, Smruti came up with the idea to work for her dad for a little while. She learned so much from him as a kid. *How much more could I learn as his employee?* she wondered. But Sri wasn't sure. He believed in Smruti, but he didn't want work to get in the way of their relationship. So Smruti's first order of business was successfully convincing her dad they could be employees at work and a loving father and daughter at home.

Smruti started at the bottom of Supreme Creations. She took on all the least glamorous jobs, like answering phones and wrapping packages. As Smruti learned the business, she also came up with a great idea. While packing and posting stacks of plain bags, Smruti started imagining bags with bright colours and bold patterns. *We could make sustainability fun*, she thought.

When Smruti shared the idea with her dad, he was excited. Smruti's idea helped the company become one of the largest of its kind in the UK. Years later, Smruti became CEO, with her dad overseeing Supreme Creations as chairman of the board of directors. Smruti thinks it's funny that her temporary job never ended. She's so glad she still gets to learn from "Dr. Ram" at the office and "dad" at home.

SMRUTI, BORN 1986 · DR. R. SRI, BORN 1957

INDIA AND UNITED KINGDOM

SOPHIA AND HAROLD ROBERTS

HEART SURGEONS

Growing up, Sophia Roberts loved to play the board game Operation. With a toy stethoscope dangling around her neck, she'd squint her eyes and pinch little tweezers as she removed tiny objects from a cartoon patient. If her fingers trembled as she pulled out one of the plastic pieces, the board would buzz angrily. But Sophia's hands were steady, like her dad's.

Sophia's dad Harold, or Hal, was a heart surgeon. Once, when Sophia was 11 or so, she went to the hospital to see her dad work. She was mesmerised watching Hal gracefully cut and stitch. For a few scary seconds, the patient's heart had to be stopped, but whirring machines kept their blood pumping. And then — like magic — the heart started again.

Sophia knew her dad's work was difficult and stressful, but she also saw how much it mattered. When Sophia's family went out to eat in their small Florida town, strangers constantly approached Hal. *You saved my Mum*, they'd say. Or *Thanks to you, I have more years to live*. When Sophia grew up, she wanted to make that kind of difference. So she became a surgeon too.

After she went to medical school, Sophia started training at a hospital in St. Louis. One day, Hal texted her. He had recently accepted a position at the very same hospital as Sophia, and he needed someone to assist with a complicated heart surgery.

Sophia and Hal both scrubbed up. Machines hummed and beeped. Hal turned on his favourite playlist. As the strums of an electric guitar filled the room, father and daughter took deep breaths. It was a magical moment. But once they started working, all that mattered was the patient.

After hours in the operating room, the surgery was a success. They'd saved a life. But for these two doctors, it was all just part of a day's work.

SOPHIA, BORN 1992 · HAROLD, BORN 1956

UNITED STATES OF AMERICA

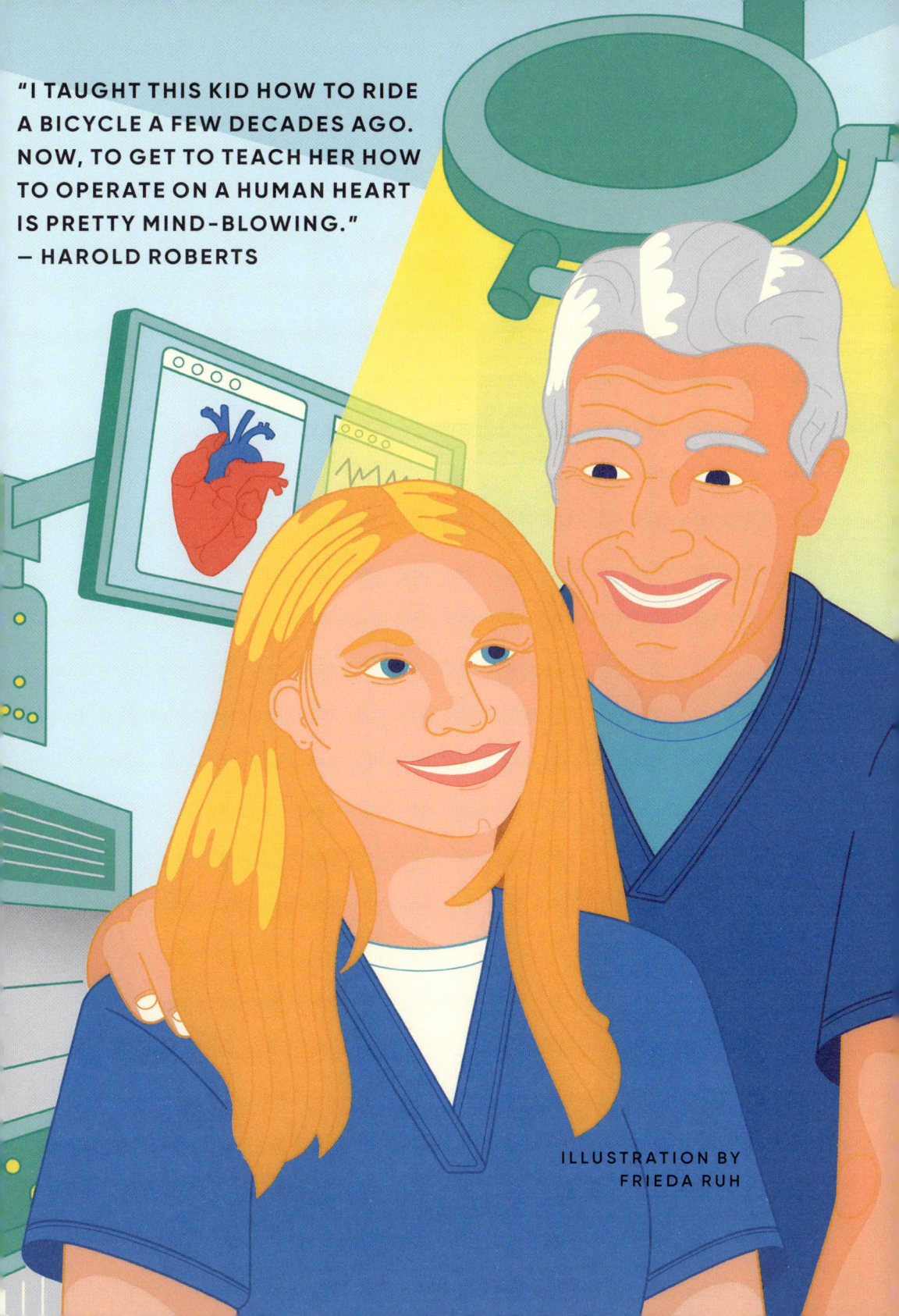

STELLA AND PAUL McCARTNEY

FASHION DESIGNER & MUSICIAN

Once upon a time there was a girl who lived two lives. Stella's dad, Paul, was a member of a famous band called the Beatles. In the '60s, the Beatles were iconic. They recorded hit after hit and sold out shows around the world. After the Beatles broke up, Paul and Linda, Stella's mum, formed a new band called Paul McCartney and Wings. As a little girl, Stella travelled on tour with the band and spent time at home in Sussex, England, on her family's farm.

"One side [of my childhood] was this farm life, and the other side was the stage, with glittery boots and glamour," Stella has said. "It was an early inspiration."

Stella watched her mum and dad rock out on stage in tailored suits, sleek boots, and wide bell-bottom jeans. At home, she tended to the family's animals and cooked plant-based meals with her parents. She didn't know it then, but both sides of her life would pave the way for her future.

When she grew up, Stella went to fashion school, and eventually started her own fashion line. But she wanted to do things a little differently. A lifelong vegetarian, she decided not to use leather or fur in any of her designs. She also made sure that her clothes were sustainably made.

When Stella and Paul teamed up on two Beatles-inspired clothing collections, their values were at the heart of the designs. Paul opened up his wardrobe for ideas, and Stella recreated pieces using sustainable materials, like a bomber jacket made from regenerated nylon instead of leather. She made colourful shirts spun with organic cotton that featured lyrics her father wrote. Together, Paul and Stella combined creative forces to make beautiful clothes with an important message.

STELLA, BORN 13 SEPTEMBER, 1971 · PAUL, BORN 18 JUNE, 1942

UNITED KINGDOM

THALMA AND LAÉRCIO DE FREITAS

MUSICIANS

Thalma sang softly as her father's hands floated over the piano keys. They were performing in a dimly lit studio. Beside them were two other musicians, Mateus Aleluia on the guitar and his daughter, Fabiana, singing as well. Thalma's dad, Laércio, looked on proudly as Thalma effortlessly hit each note. The foursome was playing the song "Cordeiro de Nanã", and the video of their voices harmonising as they sang the haunting lyrics would become iconic. Thalma didn't know that yet though. She just knew she loved to play music with her father.

It was moments like these that made Thalma realise how special it was that her dad was a musician. As a little girl growing up in the seaside city of Rio de Janeiro, she would smile proudly when people called her "the maestro's daughter."

Thalma knew she would become a performer like her dad. And when she turned 20 years old, she got her big break: she appeared in a Brazilian soap opera. While Laércio continued to compose music, Thalma acted in more than a dozen soap operas. Music, though, still called to her.

Almost 10 years later, Thalma created her first album. It was a mix of slow R&B, Brazilian sounds, and fast dance music. Then, on her second album, there was a surprise guest: Laércio.

The talented pair often performed on stage together with Laércio's skilled piano-playing accompanying Thalma's beautiful vocals. Even after decades of television appearances and multiple albums and awards between them, Thalma and Laércio cherish their memories of performing together the most.

THALMA, BORN 14 MAY, 1974 · LAÉRCIO, BORN 20 JUNE, 1941

BRAZIL

XIOMARA ROSA-TEDLA AND DAGNE TEDLA

ENTREPRENEURS

In one of Xiomara's earliest memories, her dad's luggage sat before her. He'd just got back from a trip to Ethiopia, and shimmery cloth and smooth leather goods spilled out of his suitcase. Xiomara grew up in California, but she learned so much about where her father had been from each time he returned from his visits.

By the time Xiomara was an adult with a career of her own, her dad's trips were routine. So she didn't think much of it when he came back from Ethiopia with a sleek, tan leather bag for her. But this gift was different. Everywhere she went, people stopped her to ask where she'd got it. "Oh, my dad got it for me back in Ethiopia," she'd say. Then they'd ask when he was going again, and if he could bring one back for them too! This happened so often that Dagne began to joke that they should start a business.

I already have a career, Xiomara thought. She'd got her degree in business, and was working at a big corporation. She liked certain parts of her job, but the idea of starting something new from the ground up and doing things her way was exciting. Plus, strangers on the street were already begging to buy the product!

So, in 2015, Xiomara and Dagne created their company, UnoEth. They decided to partner with artisans in Addis Ababa, Ethiopia's capital, to make handmade purses, backpacks, and wallets. Now, Xiomara and Dagne sell their products online and from a small studio in Oakland, California. When customers walk into the loft, sunshine filters in from the skylight and the Tedlas' friendly dog, Diesel, greets them. It is a family business, after all.

XIOMARA, BORN 26 JUNE, 1987 · DAGNE, BORN 12 MARCH, 1954

UNITED STATES OF AMERICA AND ETHIOPIA

ZAYA AND DWYANE WADE

MODEL AND BASKETBALL PLAYER

Zaya's heart beat fast as she gazed across the table at her dad, Dwyane, and her stepmum, Gabrielle. She took a deep breath and told them: "I'm ready to live my truth."

Zaya was 12 years old. All her life, people had told her she was a boy. But she knew deep in her heart that she was actually a girl. As she told her parents that she was transgender, her voice trembled. But as she went on, her voice got stronger and stronger.

Dwyane was glad Zaya felt safe enough to tell them. He was a retired pro basketball star, and Gabrielle was an actor, so their family was in the public eye. He promised to support and protect her.

From then on, everything changed. Their love was the same, but now, they celebrated at Pride festivals together. When haters showed up on social media, Dwyane stood up for Zaya and for LGBTQIA+ folks everywhere. It was hard sometimes, but she didn't let it bother her. She just kept living her truth.

A few years later, Zaya discovered her true passion — fashion! She loved mixing and matching bold patterns and trying out different looks. From rocking brightly coloured suits to donning sleek ball gowns, Zaya developed a sense of style all her own.

When she was 15, Zaya made her modelling debut at Paris Fashion Week. Dressed in an oversized olive blazer and a matching dress, Zaya strutted down the runway as cameras flashed. In the front row, Dwyane and Gabrielle beamed.

Later that year, Zaya made her magazine cover debut, and her dad asked for the first signed copy. Zaya scrawled her name across her cover photo. When Zaya handed it to Dwyane, he smiled at the note she'd written: *To Dad: I love you.*

ZAYA, BORN 29 MAY, 2007 · DWYANE, BORN 17 JANUARY, 1982

UNITED STATES OF AMERICA

IT'S YOUR TURN

TELL YOUR TALE

It's time to explore the Rebel you know the best — you! All you need is a piece of paper, something to write and draw with, and your imagination.

- Fold a piece of paper in half on the long end, like a book, then unfold it.

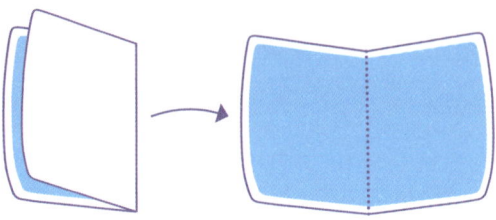

- Think about how you want to tell your story. What would you want readers to know about you if you were featured in a Rebel Girls book?
- On the left side of the fold, write your name in big, bright letters. Then, write your story.

STORYTELLING TIPS
There are lots of ways to tell your story.
- You can start with "Once upon a time..." like in Bindi and Steve Irwin's story or jump right into the action like in Coco and Corey Gauff's.
- Consider telling a story about when you were little or sharing a moment when you were extra proud of yourself.
- Make sure to add lots of details.
- If you are describing a moment in your life, close your eyes and remember what that moment was like. Then describe what it looked like, how it smelled, and the sounds you heard.

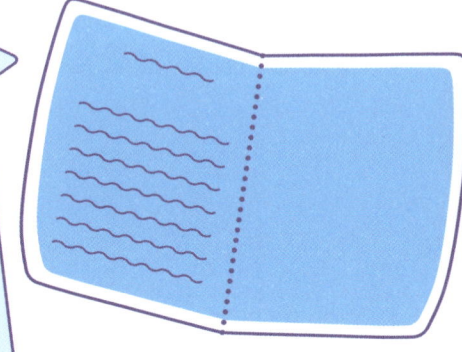

DRAW YOUR PORTRAIT

Channel your inner artist and make a self-portrait, or picture of yourself.

- What materials would you like to use? Coloured pencils? Crayons? Pens? Watercolours? Do you like to draw or paint? Gather your supplies.
- On the right side of the fold, draw your portrait.

> **UNIQUE YOU**
> Every self-portrait is different. What do you want your picture to show?
> - You can show yourself posing like Bryce Dallas Howard and Ron Howard or doing an activity like Monique and Ladi Ajayi.
> - You can focus on your face or show yourself from your head to your feet — or anything in between.
> - The portrait can be realistic or abstract, colourful or black and white — however you see yourself.
> - Don't forget the background! It can also be realistic or abstract. What does the background of your portrait show about you?

- When you're finished, you can share your story and portrait with a friend or family member, hang it up, or even keep it tucked inside this book.

MORE FUN TOGETHER!

These activities were inspired by the incredible duos you just read about. Grab your dad or other beloved grown-up and get ready to have some fun together!

GO EXPLORING

Ghazal and Qazi explore their country on their motorbikes. Together, they zoom through the mountains and cruise through towns. But guess what? You don't need motorbikes to explore your city or town with your dad! Here are a few different ways to discover interesting places near you.

- Research a nearby hiking trail or park, then lace up your trainers and get moving!
- Is there a new restaurant, ice-cream shop, or smoothie place you and your grown-up haven't tried yet? Now's the time to check it out together.
- Sometimes when you live in a place for a long time, you might forget to notice the special things about it. Take a walk through your neighbourhood with your grown-up and pay close attention to the architecture of the houses or buildings, the flowers in your neighbour's garden, or the way the trees sway in the breeze.

STORYTIME!

There are many storytellers featured in this book. Kawanabe Kyosui and Kawanabe Kyosai told stories through their paintings, and Bryce Dallas Howard and Ron Howard bring stories to life on the big screen. This activity encourages you and your grown-up to share your favourite stories. It's perfect for a rainy day!

- Each of you can pick one of your favourite books. Read the best parts to each other — or read the whole thing if it's a short book.
- Talk about what makes this story so special to you. What do you like so much about the plot, characters, or setting?
- Head to your local library or bookshop and pick out a book for both of you to read separately or together. After you've finished it, set a time to talk about what you thought of it — like a two-person book club.

SHARE SOME TUNES

Musical duos Ángela and Pepe Aguilar, Shane and Shaneyah Redstar, and Thalma and Laércio de Freitas have each performed together, sharing their deep passion for music. You don't have to be a skilled musician to enjoy this musical activity, though.

- To start, you and your grown-up will pick a favourite song to share with each other. Play each song and talk about what you like about it. Maybe it's a high-energy dance tune, and you love the way it makes you want to move. Or perhaps it's a slow song, and you're drawn to the story the lyrics tell.
- Next, pick a genre neither of you have listened to a lot before. Pick at least five songs in that genre and listen to them together. Chat about what makes this type of music unique.
- Bonus: pick a song with a simple tune that you both know well like "Happy Birthday" or "Row, Row, Row Your Boat." Keep the same melody but change the lyrics so they're about each of you. Share your new songs with each other — the sillier the better!

INTERVIEW YOUR GROWN-UP

Women like Bryce Dallas Howard, Mary-Ann Musangi, and Reata Brannaman learned a lot about their dads' careers and how they became successful by talking and spending time with them. You might think you already know a lot about your dad's job and his life before you were born, but there's always more to discover. Here are some questions you can ask over dinner, in the car, or during a quiet weekend.

- Where'd you grow up? What was the best and worst thing about it?
- What's the most interesting thing that's ever happened to you?
- What do you remember most about being my age?
- What was your favourite subject in school?
- What's the best advice you've ever received?
- When did you know you wanted to be [insert job/profession here]?
- What do you love most about your job? What do you like the least?

GET CREATIVE IN THE KITCHEN

Kathy and Peter Fang thrive in the kitchen. Their mouth-watering dishes have people flocking to their two restaurants in San Francisco. It took a long time for them to master their skills. You and your dad can start learning today.

- Do you have a sweet tooth or do you gravitate towards salty snacks? What's your favourite dish to eat for dinner? What ingredients and foods do you find delicious? Make a list!
- Compare your list with each other. Find the similarities.
- Do some research to find a simple recipe that incorporates ingredients you both enjoy, and make it together.

RESEARCH AND REPORT

Conservationist Bindi Irwin learned how to protect animals with her dad, Steve, and wildlife photographer Masayo Hiraiwa discovered nature's beauty with help from her dad, Michio. Are you and your dad or grown-up animal lovers? Take some time to learn more about the wildlife around you.

- With your grown-up, look up a list of endangered species in your county or region. Pick the one that interests you most, and have your dad pick one that is intriguing to him.
- Go online or peruse non-fiction books. Find out as much as you can about the animals you chose. What do they eat? Where do they live? Which animals are their predators? Do they live by themselves or in groups?
- Next, find out why they are endangered. Perhaps they are a marine animal that is overfished. Or maybe climate change is impacting their habitat.
- Present your findings to each other. Write an article, create a slide show, or make a poster about the animal you researched and the facts you discovered.
- Bonus: find a way to help out together! Maybe there's a birdwatching group you and your dad could take part in or an animal shelter where you could volunteer.

LISTEN TO MORE EMPOWERING STORIES ON THE REBEL GIRLS APP!

Download the app to listen to beloved Rebel Girls stories. Filled with the adventures and accomplishments of women from around the world and throughout history, the Rebel Girls app is designed to entertain, inspire, and build confidence in listeners everywhere.

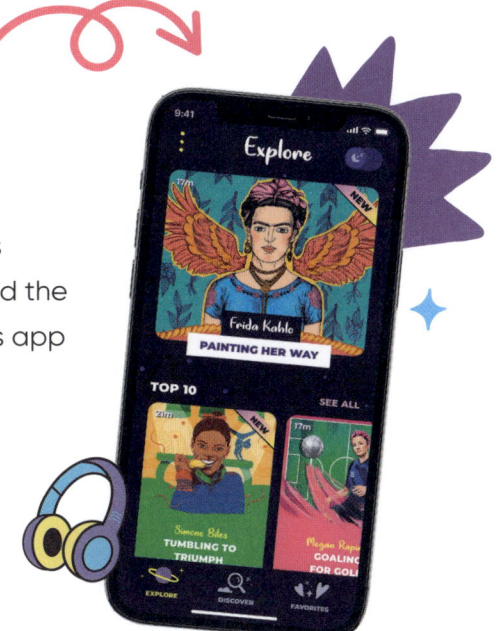

THE ILLUSTRATORS

Twenty-three extraordinary female artists from all over the world illustrated the portraits in this book.

ALLEANNA HARRIS, **USA**, 25
ANGIE ALAPE, **COLOMBIA**, 51
ARCHINA LAEZZA, **ITALY**, 7
BEATRIZ CASTRO ARBAIZAR, **SPAIN**, 41
BECE LUNA, **BRAZIL**, 11
CAITLIN RAIN, **USA**, 17
DANIELA SANCHEZ REYES, **MEXICO**, 43
FARIMAH KHAVARINEZHAD, **CANADA**, 21
FRIEDA RUH, **GERMANY**, 47
HOANG GIANG, **VIETNAM**, 31
JANEEN CONSTANTINO, **USA**, 37, 53
JUSTINE ALLENETTE ROSS, **USA**, 23

KRISTEN BRITTAIN, **USA**, 49
LENA ADDINK, **THE NETHERLANDS**, 39
MAITHILI JOSHI, **INDIA AND USA**, 45
NIKITA ABUYA, **KENYA**, 19, 33
PAULA ZORITE, **SPAIN**, 15
PEILIN LI, **CHINA**, 29
PRINCESS KARIBO, **NIGERIA AND UK**, 13
QU LAN, **FRANCE**, 35
SALINI PERERA, **CANADA**, 9
TAINA LAYLA CUNION, **USA**, 55
YIQING GAN, **MALAYSIA**, 27

MORE BOOKS!

For more stories about amazing women and girls, check out other Rebel Girls books.

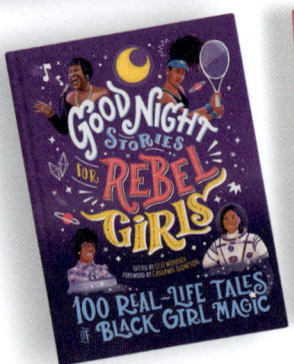
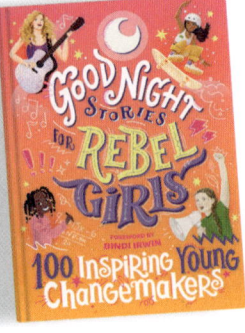

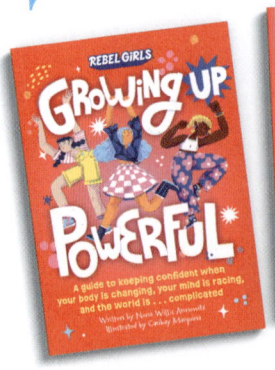

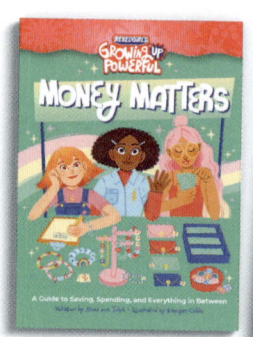

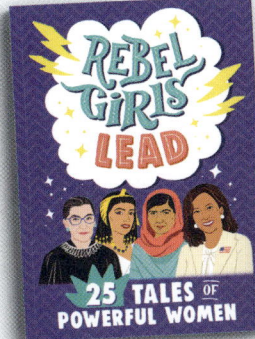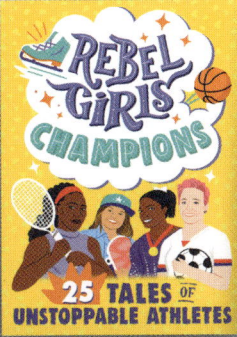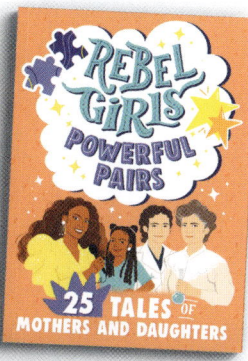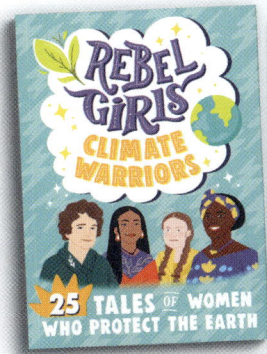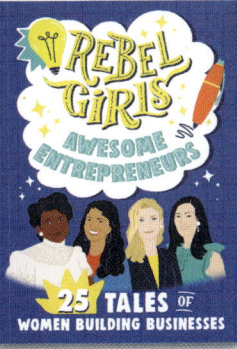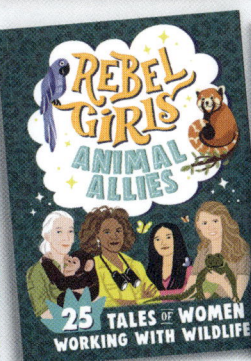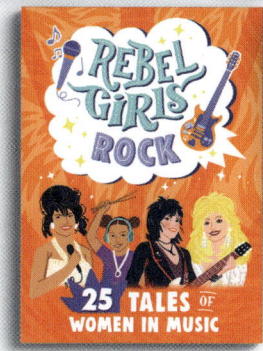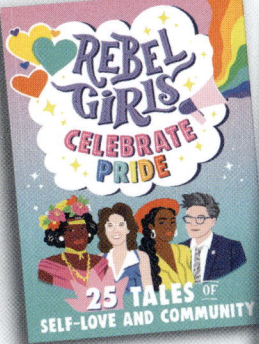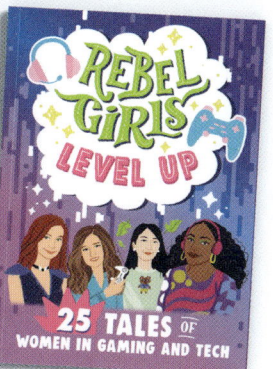

ABOUT REBEL GIRLS

REBEL GIRLS, a certified B Corporation, is a global, multi-platform empowerment brand dedicated to helping raise the most inspired and confident generation of girls through content, experiences, products, and community. Originating from an international best-selling children's book, Rebel Girls amplifies stories of real-life, extraordinary women throughout history, geography, and field of excellence. With a growing community of 30 million self-identified Rebel Girls spanning more than 100 countries, the brand engages with Generation Alpha through its book series, premier app and audio content, events, and merchandise. To date, Rebel Girls has sold more than 11 million books in 50 languages and reached 40 million audio listens. Award recognition includes the *New York Times* bestseller list, the 2022 Apple Design Award for Social Impact, multiple Webby Awards for family & kids and education, and Common Sense Media Selection honours, among others.

As a B Corp, we're part of a global community of businesses that meet high standards of social and environmental impact.

JOIN THE REBEL GIRLS COMMUNITY!
Visit rebelgirls.com and join our email list for exclusive sneak peeks, promos, activities, and more. You can also email us at hello@rebelgirls.com.

- YouTube: youtube.com/RebelGirls
- App: rebelgirls.com/audio
- Podcast: rebelgirls.com/podcast
- Facebook: facebook.com/rebelgirls
- Instagram: @rebelgirls
- Email: hello@rebelgirls.com
- Web: rebelgirls.com

If you liked this book, please take a moment to review it wherever you prefer!